Aguantaelhambre and the Other East L.A. Legends Ch1-8

Chapter 1: El Rancho en el Barrio

Chapter 2: Aguantaelhambre

Chapter 3: The Dumbass Dalmation

Chapter 4: Pirate and the Dog Party Crew

Chapter 5: Tyson the Ear Biter

Chapter 6: Lobo, el Guardián

Chapter 7: Budweiser: The Goat

Chapter 8: The Ones Who Didn't Make It

Chapter 9: Duck Duck Revenge

Chapter 10: Soccer Sundays

Chapter 11: Los Camarones

Chapter 12: Bola de Fak Yus

Chapter 13: La Araña – The Mexican Classic

Chapter 14: The Moco Mobile

Chapter 15: Leaving Jaime at the Drive-In

Chapter 16: Cheeseburgers for the Homeless

Chapter 17: Alfonso and the Nail-Biting Cure

Chapter 18: Pa'l Alex

Chapter 19: La Barca Tips

Chapter 20: Salt Shakers

Chapter 21: Diesel – The Multi-Purpose Home Tool

Chapter 22: Philly Fish

Chapter 23: Sandía Sale

Chapter 24: Mi Tío Manuel, el de las Paletas

Chapter 25: Ha Vale

Chapter 26: Oh My Dara

Chapter 27: A mi no me digas So

Chapter 28: No Me Truenen los Dientes

Chapter 29: Superman

Chapter 30: Sopatelas

Chapter 31: Las Reinas del Fútbol

Chapter 32: Caramelo

Chapter 33: Our Room

Chapter 34: Mismatched and Mole

Where do I Start:

That question still hits me. Where do I start?

I grew up surrounded by noise; barking, honking, yelling, music.

We didn't have much, but we had stories.

We had dogs with names and legends.

We had chaos.

We had life.

We had mismatched forks and mole jars for cups.

We had bunk beds in closets, cot mattresses we thought were luxury, and pizza pans "borrowed" from Shakey's.

We had rules like "don't say 'so,'" and punishments that involved kneeling upright on cold tile while trying not to cry.

We had laughs.

We had chancla dodgeball.

We had love.

And somehow, through all that madness, we turned out okay.

I still laugh about Firu.

I still miss Lobo.

I still think about Pirata running with the crew like he had a curfew.

Growing up poor wasn't a tragedy. We didn't even know we were poor. My mom did an incredible job of hiding it and even if she hadn't, we were too busy laughing, running, sneaking Shakey's dishes, and building forts in rooms the size of closets.

It was messy.

It was loud.

It was beautiful.

It was home.

Aguantaelhambre and the Other East L.A. Legends

Chapter 1: El Rancho en el Barrio

Where do I even start? Our house in East L.A. wasn't just home; it was a zoo, a rancho, and sometimes a battlefield. We didn't need to go to the L.A. Zoo to see animals. We had our own petting zoo, minus the rules. Rabbits, chickens, ducks, geese, goats; they all came and went through that front yard. The whole block knew us as the house with the barking, clucking, honking soundtrack. And somehow, it was normal to us.

Feeding the animals was a daily mission, and usually that mission got passed to me. My mom would hand me a plato of food and tell me to go feed the chickens and geese. I'd walk out there, throw the scraps, and run like hell. Those cabrones would chase me like I owed them money. The geese were the worst. They'd puff up their chests and charge like they owned the place. It was survival of the fastest.

But there was something beautiful about the chaos. This was my version of home. We didn't have a lot of money, but we had a lot of life. And that yard, as wild as it was, had more personality than most people I knew.

Chapter 2: Aguantaelhambre

Our first real dog that I remember was "Aguantaelhambre".

His name? Self-explanatory.

Poor guy probably hadn't eaten right since birth. It became a running joke; "Did anyone feed Aguantaelhambre?"

He'd just be out there, chillin', skinny as hell, looking at you like, *"Help me, pendejo. Dame de tragar."*

But he was tough. Resilient. East L.A. tough.

As far as I know, he's still buried in the backyard under the carport, but I don't know for sure. Could've been under the lemon tree, or maybe by the cinder blocks. Either way, he became legend. Aguantaelhambre was the beginning of a long line of neighborhood dogs who came through our lives, left paw prints, and sometimes, never left at all.

Chapter 3: The Dumbass Dalmatian

El Firu. Now there was a dog with no loyalty and no sense. A dalmatian with all spots and zero brains. He'd bolt every time the door cracked open. Not just run down the street; he'd be *gone*. Like trying to catch a ghost with four legs.

Our friend Oscar Ibarra once found him about a half mile away on Gage and Brooklyn by the hardware store, just walking like he belonged there. I remember one time I was heading out to a mariachi gig. Full charro suit. Pulling the car out and—*bam*—Firu fucking escapes. I'm chasing him down the street in my traje, looking like a telenovela gone wrong. Monday morning at school, one of my students Sammy, smirks and says, "Hey, what did you do this weekend?" I responded with, "Nothing." He says, "You sure? You didn't have a mariachi chamba? I saw you chasing your dog this weekend." I was so embarrassed. I told him, "I'll give you extra credit if you don't tell anyone else." He agreed and we never spoke of it again.

Chapter 4: Pirata and the Dog Party Crew

Pirata was a Christmas gift from my neighbor and honorary Grandma Lolly. He had this black patch over one eye, like a pirate, so the name stuck. He was supposed to be big and bad ass dog; part pit bull, part St. Bernard, but the dude never grew. Still, he had the biggest heart.

He used to wait for me every night when I got back from work, sometimes at 3 or 4 in the morning. As soon as I pulled up to the house, there he'd be at the gate, wagging his tail like I was his whole world. But Pirata also had a social life. The neighborhood dogs would roll up in a pack, standing across the street like, *"Let's go, bro. The bitches are waiting."* And Pirata would give me the look, *"C'mon, man. Go inside already."* Sometimes I did. I'd just open the gate and let him run off. He always came back. Once, I caught him mid-sneak coming through the alley. He looked at me like, *"Shit. I'm Busted"* and ran back inside the yard. I walked in the house as fast as I could so that he wouldn't miss his date.

Chapter 5: Tyson the Ear Biter

Tyson. Named not because he was strong, but because he once tried to bite my dad's ear off. Straight up Tyson vibes, about a week after Mike Tyson bit off part of Evander Holyfield's ear. He wasn't the smartest, but he was loyal. My mom didn't really care for him much. Didn't give him enough attention, but he still stuck around like a soldier.

Tyson wasn't flashy.

He didn't have a dramatic story.

But he was always there.

And sometimes, that's more than enough.

Chapter 6: Lobo, el Guardián

Lobo was the first dog I ever loved. Big, loyal, protective. If my dad raised his voice or his hand at us, Lobo was there in a flash. Growling. Standing between us. Sometimes, my dad would have us lie down on the ground and make him jump over us. My dad took credit for training him to jump so far, but because he loved us Lobo didn't want to land on us.

When he got old, he couldn't walk well. He started losing weight. Instead of putting him down the right way, because my father would never spend any money on a vet, my mom and Alfonso took him to the railroad tracks by my grandma's and left him there. Just left him. That shit still messes me up. He was family. And he deserved better. I used to tell my parents that when they got old and senile, I was going to do the same to them.

Chapter 7: Budweiser: The Goat

Growing up in East L.A. in the 80s, there was never a dull moment. Living next door to cholos meant two things: there was always drama, and there were always bargains. And I mean *bargains*. One day, when I was about seven, they sold my dad a goat. Not just any goat. A goat named Budweiser. My pops dropped a crisp hundred dollars on that beast. I'm pretty sure it was either stolen or swapped in some weird underground livestock deal, but to us, it was a new family member.

Except Budweiser didn't act like family. He acted like a prison guard with horns. That goat was more territorial than our dogs. I could barely get into the yard without a full-blown showdown. I'd inch toward the gate and Budweiser would rise up on his hind legs, eyes locked on me, and slam his head into the chain link like I owed him money. I had to use distraction techniques just to make it across the yard. Most days, I'd throw something in one direction and make a mad dash to the porch, leaping over our little gate like it was the Olympic trials.

Most of the time, Budweiser was chained to the fence, pacing and snorting like a caged bull. But every once in a while, my dad would decide it was a good idea to let him loose and tell *me* to go tie him back up. That became a mission straight out of a farm show. I'd sneak up on him with the rope in hand, only to get smacked with a headbutt so strong it'd knock me on my ass. If cell phones had been around back then, I'm convinced I'd have been a viral sensation; "Kid Gets Bullied by Goat."

We had Budweiser for about a year. Then one day, my dad decided it was time for him to serve a higher purpose; dinner. He called Don Nico, our neighbor across the street. Don Nico was an old-school dude who knew how to cook meat the *real* way: in a traditional underground pit. It was decided Budweiser was going to be birria.

I remember the day like a movie. Don Nico came over, grabbed Budweiser, and calmly walked him next door to the corner of Floral and Brannick. Our neighbors had a bigger tree, perfect for the job. They tied his legs together and hoisted him up. And then it happened, Don Nico slit Budweiser's throat. That goat *screamed*. I mean, people driving by were rubbernecking so hard they almost crashed. It was chaos.

He cut off the head; screams still echoing somehow, and started skinning him like it was just a regular day. To my young mind, it was brutal and kinda fascinating. Then Budweiser got chopped into pieces and placed into a giant tin can for the pit.

Eight hours later, we were all sitting around the table, plates piled high with birria, dipping tortillas, and smacking our lips. I didn't know whether to feel guilty or grateful. All I knew was, it was delicious.

That was East L.A. in the 80s. No filters. No warning labels. Just life. Raw, loud, and unforgettable.

Chapter 8: The Ones Who Didn't Make It

We had a lot of puppies over the years. Most didn't survive. It was rough. We didn't always have money for vet visits or proper food. And my dad, man, he could be cold. If a litter wasn't looking good, he'd put them in a bag and make my brother dump them near the 60 freeway onramp off of Floral Dr. I still think about the people who lived there. How many mornings they woke up to the horror of finding a black trash bag with dead puppies. Pinche brujeria, they must have thought.

It's one of those East L.A. stories you don't brag about. Just part of what made us tough, and sometimes, numb.

Chapter 9: Duck Duck Revenge

We had a pit bull puppy once, and a duck and three geese that used to mess with him constantly. Pecking at him, taunting him like bullies at recess. He was tied up and couldn't fight back.

Back then, our dogs spent most of their time tied up to the clothes line with a chain around their neck. We didn't have kennels and since that was the norm, nobody called animal control to report it as cruelty.

One day, we came home and the yard looked like a crime scene. Dog was loose. Duck and geese? Laid out, necks snapped. I know it's messed up, but honestly, I felt a little satisfaction. Payback. Justice for all the bites and pecks, not only to the dog but to me. I think my mom had fun watching me try to feed the geese. She would send me out with the scraps and as I would approach their feeding station, they would circle around me and peck at my heels. They looked like cobras snapping their necks back and forth chasing me around the yard as I tried to make it back in the house.

Chapter 10: Soccer Sundays

Every freaking Sunday. Like clockwork. My dad made us wake up early to go watch our uncles play soccer. Rain or shine, flu or feria, didn't matter—¡*vámonos!* Off we went to some dusty-ass park in South Central L.A. to cheer on a bunch of grown men acting like they were in the damn World Cup.

And it was always the same story: We'd pull up in the beat up Dodge Dart, Brady bunch station wagon or the Moco Mobile, sit on the damn floor, maybe eat some pan dulce if we were lucky, and watch my Rodrigo miss every shot he took while my Tio Manuel slowly turned into Cantinflas con cerveza.

By halftime, he was twelve beers in and talking shit to everyone. By full-time, he was ready to fight.

And then came the real horror: **the ride home.**

If somebody passed us up on the freeway—
oh hell no. Suddenly my dad would grip the
wheel, puff out his chest like he was Vin
Diesel, and say, "*¡Yo también tengo!*" and
slam the gas in the old Gran Torino migra
car he bought at auction.

That car was cursed, man. The first time we
pulled up anywhere in it, people legit
freaked out and started to run. They thought
it was the migra until they realized my dad
was driving. It didn't help that my dad left it
the original migra mint green with the white
top. The back doors didn't open from the
inside, and one of the windows was jammed
halfway down. The whole thing smelled like
sweat and old fries.

After a while, Sundays lost their sparkle. It
was the same story every week. Eventually,
I learned how to drive, which was both a
blessing and a punishment. Because guess
who became the official drunk-dad
chauffeur? This pendejo right here. My
brothers although older, were excused to not
join us on Sunday's under the demise that,
"We have homework."

My mom would hit me with the guilt trip:

"No me dejes sola, mijo. Tú maneja. Ándale, por favor. Yo te pago."

My dad even had the huevos to let everyone know he could drink as much as he wanted (not that anything stopped him before).

"Aqui tengo mi taxi." With great pride as if I did it for him.

And just like that, there went the pendejo behind the wheel. Mind you, I was in the 8th grade at the time, con la licencia de Dios.

So yeah. Soccer Sundays. A little fútbol. A lotta trauma.

Chapter 11: Los Camarones

Weekend routines were the norm for us. For some time, it was going to "los camarones" for breakfast. My mom would get us out of bed at 8 in the morning, partially because she didn't want to cook and partially because she wanted my dad to spend some money on us. We'd roll out somewhere off San Pedro St and 24th to chase down shrimp guy.

Not at a restaurant. Not even a taco truck. Nah, this guy was slanging cocteles straight out the back of his station wagon. He had ice chests in the trunk packed with shrimp, octopus, jaiva, you name it. Clamato, cucumbers, onion, all the fixings. People would pull up, place their order like it was a drive-thru, and bounce.

If you didn't get there early, you were shit out of luck.

No shrimp for you.

He'd run out fast. My dad acted like it was some secret treasure map he found.

"Nobody knows about this spot," he'd say. Yeah right, Dad—there's fifteen cars already in line and why the fuck you think this guy runs out early? It was a great coctel and wasn't a secret that could be kept for long.

Eventually, the man leveled up. Got himself a real truck, parked it by the Napa Auto Parts over on Washington and Griffith Ave. Had signs and everything. But you know how it goes—prices went up, portions got smaller, and that original magic kinda disappeared.

We stopped going. But man, for those first few weekends, it felt like a mission. Like we were part of something underground.

Chapter 12: Bola de Fak Yus

One time we were riding around with my Tío Daniel. My Tio always packed his van full of people, like we were going on tour or something. These were the times when there were no seatbelt laws or in his vans case there were no seatbelts. A bunch of my drunk tios were in the van along with this guy they called *El Bisco*.

So we're packed into this van, heading to San Gabriel to find the guy who sells Tejuino on Rosemead in Pico Rivera. All of a sudden, Bisco falls off his seat and somehow hits his face on something. I don't remember what happened exactly, but the dude ended up with a chingo of blood all over his face and shirt, looking like he was in a boxing match with his arms tied behind his back. Instead of helping him, they let him lay there on the van floor bleeding (he was passed out drunk). When we got back to the house, the women started screaming when they saw him stumble out of the back of the van with his shirt soaked in blood. Someone told his wife, "Unos negros le dieron en la madre. Se lo chingaron."

Bisco comes to, still out of it, and immediately starts popping off. *"Bola de fak yus!"* he yells, eyes still half shut and face all crusty with blood.

"Me la van a pagar todos ustedes! Ustedes son una bola de FakYus. No me ayudaron."

He's throwing out threats like he's the Godfather pointing at people like he's calling a lineup. Nobody even knew what he was talking about, but we were dying laughing.

That's how it was though. Half drama, half comedy. You never knew if you were about to witness a fight, a novela, or a stand-up routine. Sometimes, it was all three.

Chapter 13: La Araña – The Mexican Classic

My dad had this old Dodge Dart, and I swear every Mexican family on the block had one too. It was like a rite of passage—before you could afford a carro del ano, you had to put in your years with a Dart. He called it *La Araña*—no idea why, but it stuck.

That thing was a beast. The paint was faded, the upholstery was shot, and it made noises that didn't sound street legal. But my dad loved it like it was a lowrider straight outta Whittier Boulevard.

I remember one time when my dad came home drunk—nothing new—but this time, *La Araña* had a big-ass dent in the fender. No explanation, just "pinche árbol se atravesó."

Next thing you know, we're outside in the dark with a hammer and a two-by-four, like we're part of the pit crew at the junkyard 500. I'm holding the wood while he's banging away at the car like he's fixing a fence. No body shop, no insurance. Just puro ingenio Mexicano and vibes.

And you know what? It kind of worked. The dent wasn't gone, but it was less embarrassing. That Dart lived to see another five years of desmadre.

Some people had nice cars.

We had *La Araña*.

Chapter 14: The Moco Mobile

This one was legendary in its own right—*The Moco Mobile*.

My dad showed up with in one Saturday and told us he bought it at an auction. It was a Gran Torino looking like it just finished a shift at the border. Still painted mint green with the white top. Only thing missing was the logo and lights.

Alfonso ended up buying it off him, and just like that, it became our official ride to Garfield High.

Bright green and impossible to miss, all of our friends knew it. Some called it *The Green Hornet*, but most of us just called it what it was—the Moco.

The thing was a straight-up death trap. You'd hit the brakes, and instead of slowing down, the car got faster. Like it got mad you were trying to stop it. You had to pump the brakes like you were playing a damn accordion just to get it to hesitate. And when you stepped on the pedal, your leg would just sink into the floor like you were stepping into a pothole.

But hey, not to complain. That crusty green beast got us where we needed to go. Kinda. Sorta. Most of the time. It was 1987 when we decided we would drive it to Sacramento. Alfonso, Miguel and I were part of the Sacramento Freelenacers Drum and Bugle Corps and because we had a performance that Friday night for the debut of Stand and Deliver, we decided we would drive the moco and meet up with the corp. What a mistake that was, but then again I wouldn't be sharing that story now. It was the three of us and David "Patch" driving up the 5 freeway. When we got to Valencia, close to Magic Mountain, the car started acting up, like it was trying to catch it's wind, almost as if saying slow down fuckers I can't breathe. Like when your tia climbs 2 stairs. We pulled over on the side of the freeway, walking around the car like we knew what the fuck we were doing. Popped the hood and nothing looked out of place and no smoke or anything. We let it sit for about 5 minutes, turned it on and it started, so we jumped back in like pendejos and said vamonos. About 15 minutes from then, I was woken up by Alfonso's yelling. "Get up fuckers. You need to help us push." I looked up all groggy and saw that Patch was running along side the drivers door, steering through the window and Alfonso on the front passenger side. I opened the back door and jumped out running while trying to wake up Miguel. We were rolling down hill, so we weren't really pushing the car. Miguel steps out of the car and as soon as his feet hit the asphalt, so did his body. I just remember seeing him fade out in the darkness as we kept rolling forward. Patch who was on the other side didn't know Miguel had fallen out of the car and freaked out when he saw a white t-shirt and white shoes running behind the car. It was pitch black and Miguel was very dark skinned. Patch almost steered the car off the shoulder because he thought a ghost was chasing us. At this point, I had stopped "pushing" the car and was on the side of the road laughing my ass off. The car eventually rolled to a stop and Miguel finally caught up to us. We were able to start the car again and drove it off the freeway to a mechanic next the Denny's before the grapevine.

The mechanic said it would be about an hour and suggested we go eat at Denny's across the street. We did and since we didn't have much cash, Alfonso, Patch and I ordered the $3.99 special. The waiter asks Miguel what he wants and the bastard orders a steak, well done. We were looking at him, like, "Ah Cabron. Steak well done. No quiere nada este guey." Then he has the balls to ask if they had anything to drink like Kool-Aid, because he didn't want to waste money. When the bill gets there, he tries to pitch in $5. Pendejo. His meal was more expensive than the rest of us.

The mechanic said it was the carburetor and was able to fix it so that we could get to our destination. I don't know why we didn't just turn back since we were an hour from home instead of driving the extra 5 to Sacramento. Alfonso starts with his, "Sacramento or bust." So ay vamos como pendejos. We eventually rolled up to the rehearsal in Sacramento at 7am as everyone was waking up. With the car turning off on us every hour or so and us having to let it cool down, the trip took us about 9 hours. While we were there for the weekend, Patch did some Mexican engineering and was able to "fix" the carburetor with some goop and an aluminum can. I don't know if Alfonso ever got it fixed correctly or just kept it going the way it was.

Chapter 15: Leaving Jaime at the Drive-In

When I was in junior high, my brothers and friends used to hit up the Fiesta 4 drive-in over in Pico all the time. It was kind of our weekend spot, especially since money was tight and we could sneak into the movies without paying. Five or six of us would cram into David's nova and a block before getting there, we would hide in the trunk so that they wouldn't charge us. David even changed his voice with a heavy paisa accent. "Guan Teeket Plis." They must have thought he was some perv or lonely fucker going to watch a movie in his car all alone.

Since there wasn't room for all of us inside the car, we'd bring out the folding chairs and post up in front of the car with the boom box. Ghetto surround sound.

One night, we were all hanging out, watching the movie, and I noticed the crowd was getting smaller. I looked up and saw that everyone was sitting in the car except Jaime and I. He was all into the movie and didn't notice when I jumped in the car.

Poor dude was still sitting out there by himself, surrounded by our chairs, snacks, jackets; just kicking back like the loneliest moviegoer. David put the car in reverse and started honking as we drove away just so people would turn and look at him.

He tried getting in the car, but we drove away and left him there.

We circled the lot and came back, and Jaime was *pissed.* Like, steam-coming-out-his-ears pissed.

Everyone was laughing at him. He jumped in the car, didn't say a word, but you could feel the rage radiating off him.

On the way home, he was riding shot gun with a big ol' bag of ice and just started throwing chunks at random people on the street. No warning, just *whap*. He hit one dude who was standing next to a Corvette. Not even a regular car, a Corvette.

Bad move. The guy jumps in and starts chasing us, and now we're all in panic mode. We're thinking this dude's strapped or something. He's by himself, we're like five deep, and somehow he's still scarier.

We're flying down the street in *George*, David's Nova, thinking we can outrun a Corvette. Spoiler alert: we couldn't. The guy pulls up next to us, winds down his window, and chucks a coffee cup straight into the car. David had his window down, and that cup smacked the dash and exploded like a mocha grenade.

Once we realized we weren't about to get shot or arrested, we all just started laughing our asses off.

Classic Jaime.

Chapter 16: Cheeseburgers for the Homeless

Back when Jack in the Box was running that two for 99 cent cheeseburger deal, we had a tradition. We'd roll up, order thirty cheeseburgers—*treinta*, just like that—and stack 'em up in the backseat like we were feeding an army.

At first, yeah, we'd eat a bunch ourselves—who wouldn't? But the real fun started after we were full. We'd cruise downtown with the leftovers and hand them out to the homeless. Only, we didn't exactly do it the polite way. Nah. We'd roll down the window and *airmail* those burgers. Tossing them gently (well, sometimes gently) to people on the sidewalk. "¡Ahí te va, jefe!"

Some of them caught it like pros. Others got hit in the chest with a warm cheeseburger surprise. It wasn't the classiest way to give, but we were broke kids trying to do something right in our own messed-up way. They appreciated it, though. Some even waited for us the next time.

The best part? We'd go right back to Jack's like we were starting fresh.

"Yeah, can we get thirty more cheeseburgers?"

Speaking of Jacks, our go to was the one on Brooklyn (now Cesar Chavez) and Eastern. Sometimes just for kicks, we would place giant orders without intending to pay for them. The drive through there had an opening that led to the parking lot. After we ordered, we would just cut to the parking lot and watch as the confusion unfolded.

The workers would hand the massive order to the next car, and you'd just see confused faces like, *"I didn't order all this shit!"* Sometimes arguments would ensue with the workers accusing the drivers of ordering food without the intention of paying. They would look out the window trying to figure out who ordered, but we never got caught.

We were cracking up, watching from the lot, seeing the whole thing unfold. We weren't trying to waste food—half the time we'd circle back and grab it ourselves. But man, it was funny. One of those dumb teenage things that made no sense, but somehow made all the sense in the world at the time.

And yeah, we could've been a little more respectful handing out the burgers, but we meant well. Feeding people, laughing with each other, just being creative with our time.

Even now, every time I drive past a Jack in the Box, I think: *thirty cheeseburgers please.*

Chapter 17: Alfonso and the Nail-Biting Cure

Alfonso used to bite his nails like it was his job. Like he was getting paid per finger. It didn't matter where we were; church, a party, the car;; if he had a free hand, it was going straight to his mouth.

My mom hated it. "Te vas a tragar los dedos, Alfonso," she'd say. She tried everything; slapping his hand, yelling at him, guilt-tripping him in front of guests. Nothing worked.

But then one day, she came up with a master plan. The kind of plan only a Latina mom could invent.

"¿Sabes qué?" she told me, "Te voy a poner cagada en los dedos." I thought she was joking.

She wasn't.

She came into the room holding a cold glass of water like she was just getting him a drink. All chill. Then, *bam!* She grabbed his hand and shoved his finger in it.

"¡Ay, guácala!" Alfonso started gagging instantly. Like full-body dry heaving. He took off running to the bathroom and nearly knocked the door off the hinges. You could hear him throwing up from the bedroom.

After that? Never saw his fingers in his mouth again. One traumatic splash and boom; cured. My mom was walking around like she just won a Nobel Prize for Mexican parenting.

She tried to pull the same thing on me. Gave me the same speech, told me she'd do it if I didn't stop. I laughed it off. Still bite my nails to this day. Guess I needed the cold-water special, too.

But man, that moment is burned into my memory forever.

The look on Alfonso's face.

The sudden betrayal.

The gagging.

We talk about it every family gathering like it's folklore now.

Chapter 18: Pa'l Alex

Every time we went out to eat on the weekends, it somehow turned into a detour to one of my uncle's houses. Like clockwork. For a while, the go-to spot was my Tío Filo's pad over on Washington and Vermont. We'd hit up the camarones truck or sometimes head to La Barca on Vermont if we were feeling fancy; or at least as fancy as we could get with a group of loud, hungry Mexican kids.

But here's the part that still cracks me up.

Instead of leaving the extra crackers at the restaurant like normal people, my dad would scoop them up and say, "*Llévatelas pa'l Alex.*" Every single time. Alex was one of their godsons, just a little guy back then, maybe three years old. And apparently, he was the designated cracker recipient.

Now imagine that. You're a little kid, and your *padrinos* show up to visit you. You're probably thinking, "Oh snap! They brought me a toy!" Nah. What you get instead? A handful of stale-ass saltine crackers. Like it's Christmas and Lent rolled into one.

I used to think, man, how sad is that? Who wants to get hyped over dry crackers? But then again, Alex never turned them down. Not once. Which says a lot. Either he really liked crackers, or what he had at home made saltines feel like filet mignon.

I always said if I were my uncle, I'd be pissed. You're showing up to my house with restaurant leftovers for my kid? Not even a coctel to dip them in? Come on, man. Give the kid a chance. At least get him some shrimp to go with the salt.

Still, that became part of our tradition. We'd feast, grab the extras, and make sure little Alex got his delivery. One time I swear we walked in with like ten packets of crackers in my dad's pocket. That was the gift. My dad had this proud look like he just brought gold to the house.

Years later, we still joke about it. "Pa'l Alex," we say anytime someone tries to give away their leftovers. And honestly, I think those crackers were just an excuse. It wasn't about the food. It was about showing up, being present, sharing even the smallest thing.

Still, I hope someone eventually bought the kid a damn Happy Meal.

Chapter 19: La Barca Tips

Talking about La Barca, that was one of our go-to spots. If we weren't at the camarones, we were sitting in a booth at La Barca on Vermont, ordering the usual and making ourselves way too comfortable.

My dad; man, bless his heart, he always tried to do the right thing. Every time we finished eating, he'd leave a tip. But I'm talking like two, maybe three bucks. And this wasn't some quiet weekday visit. Nah, this was the whole squad rolling in on the weekend, loud, hungry, and posted up like we owned the place.

Now that I'm older, I get it. The waitresses probably *hated* when they saw us coming through the door. And now I understand why sometimes we had to wait forever for a table, even when half the restaurant was empty. I'm pretty sure they were in the back flipping coins to see who got stuck with our table. "Not it!" "Hell no, I did them last Sunday!"

But here's the real kicker.

When we were done eating and it was time to go, Alfonso and I had our own little mission. We'd tell our parents, "Oh, we have to go to the bathroom," like clockwork. But we weren't going to pee; we were going to snatch the tip off the table.

Yup. We'd race each other to see who could get to it first.

Sometimes we split it.

Sometimes we fought over it.

But every time, that poor little tip never made it to the waitress. My dad would walk out thinking he left his two bucks, and the waitress would come back to a clean table and no change.

Looking back, I feel bad. Not just for the waitress, but for my dad. He probably already looked like a cheap bastard with that two-dollar tip, and now it was completely gone? Man. No wonder they always brought us cold tortillas and forgot the salsa.

A couple of crumpled bills felt like treasure back then.

Moral of the story? Tip your servers. And if you're gonna raise little thieves, make sure they aim higher than two bucks.

Chapter 20: Salt Shakers

For a while, Alfonso and I were on a mission. A stupid one, but a mission nonetheless. Everywhere we went, diners, taco joints, sit-down restaurants, even our kitchen, we had one goal: untwist the tops of the salt shakers.

Sometimes we did it right when we sat down, just for the thrill. But most of the time, we waited until we were leaving, setting a trap for the next poor soul who just wanted a little extra flavor. Unscrew the cap, twist it back on just enough to sit there innocent, and walk away like nothing happened.

We thought we were slick. Little saboteurs with baby faces and bad intentions. No one ever saw us do it, or if they did, they didn't say anything. But one day, karma caught up.

We were at some restaurant. I don't even remember which one, and I went to salt my food like normal. I didn't even think about it. I lifted the shaker, gave it a shake, and— *SAS!* A full avalanche of salt came crashing down onto my plate. Looked like someone dumped a bag of coke on my beans and rice.

I just stared at it in shock, and Alfonso started cracking up.

"Bro, I already got that one," he said, tears in his eyes.

I couldn't even be mad. I did the same thing all the time. I just scraped off as much salt as I could, looked around to make sure no one saw, and ate the damn food like it was all part of the plan.

We never got caught, but looking back, I wonder how many people cursed our names under their breath.

How many perfectly good enchiladas were ruined because two little mocosos thought they were being hilarious.

We didn't do it to be mean, we just thought it was funny. Harmless, childish desmadre. But man, when you're the one staring at a salt pile the size of a small hill, it doesn't feel so harmless.

Still, I think about that day every time I touch a salt shaker now. Always check the lid first. Lesson learned. The hard way.

Chapter 21: Diesel – The Multi-Purpose Home Tool

At our house, diesel was the answer to everything. Forget Raid or Roundup or lighter fluid—my dad had one solution, and it came in a recycled jug that stunk up the whole yard.

Ant problem? "Use diesel."

Weed problem? "Use diesel."

Charcoal not lighting? You already know.

I remember being handed that old gallon jug; no label, just a piece of duct tape slapped on the side, and told to go out back and take care of the ant problem. Most kids had spray cans with safety caps and pleasant lemony scents. I had straight-up industrial fumes leaking onto my sneakers. I'd walk around the yard, barefoot half the time, pouring trails of diesel like I was setting up for a bonfire, and breathing it in like it was Vicks.

No wonder I always had a headache growing up. I was basically getting high off diesel at age eight and didn't even know it.

My dad made it seem like diesel was this magical elixir. Once, we were getting ready for a backyard carne asada and ran out of lighter fluid. No problem. He poured diesel right on the charcoal and tossed in a match. That grill lit up like the Fourth of July—
WHOOSH!

Flames shot up so high I thought they were gonna catch the laundry on the clothesline.

The meat? Tasted like a mechanic's glove. But we ate it anyway. That or starve.

The day we finally gave it up was because of Alfonso, of course. He was lighting the BBQ, did it just like Dad showed him, and the flame followed the stream of diesel right back into the bottle. The whole damn jug caught on fire in his hands. My mom screamed like we were being attacked. Alfonso dropped the bottle and ran. Diesel puddled under the grill and flames danced like brujos around the patio.

After that, my mom banned diesel from the backyard. She went out and bought a bottle of actual lighter fluid and said, "No más chingaderas."

But my dad? He still found ways to sneak it into use. Spraying it on weeds like he was an exterminator with a death wish. "Ya ves. Si trabaja," he'd say. Yeah, and it also probably shaved a few years off my memory.

Sometimes I wonder how many brain cells that stuff killed off me. But hey, our yard was ant-free, the grill always lit, and the weeds didn't stand a chance.

Chapter 22: Philly Fish

Jack in the Box was one of the few drive-thrus my dad didn't mind taking us to. It wasn't fancy, but it was close, and more importantly, it had fish sandwiches. That was the magic combo.

Now, McDonald's had the Filet-O-Fish, but Jack had something else entirely: the Moby Jack. Try explaining *that* to my dad, especially after he'd been drinking.

We'd pull into the drive-thru, the speakers crackling with static, and my dad would lean over and shout with full confidence, "Un Philly Fish."

The cashier would pause, confused. "What was that?"

"Un Philly Fish!" he'd repeat, louder this time, like volume would suddenly make it exist on the menu.

We'd all start snickering in the back seat. David, sitting behind dad, would eventually jump in and save the day.

"He wants a Moby Jack."

We'd place the rest of the order; burgers, fries, chicken fajita pita, and roll up to the window, trying to keep a straight face while my dad looked dead serious, like he just ordered the finest fish sandwich in East L.A.

But the best part was when they would hand dad a milkshake.

"¿¡Quién ordenó esta mierda!?" he'd yell, holding up the vanilla shake like it was toxic waste.

We'd all scramble to explain, pointing fingers, making excuses. "It came with the combo!" "You said you wanted something cold!"

Didn't matter. Once he was annoyed, logic was useless. He'd keep complaining as he unwrapped the Moby Jack and took a big bite. Carmen always got lucky since she rode in the front seat with my parents, she always got the milkshake.

Even if he never got the name right, even if he cursed the milkshake every time, even if the drive-thru guy was laughing at us in the back, there was something about those weekends. Sitting in the car, windows fogged up from the food, the smell of fries and deep-fried fish filling the air.

Moby Jack or Philly Fish—whatever he called it—it was part of the ritual. Our kind of drive-thru magic.

Chapter 23: Sandía Sale

One summer, my dad's friend rolled in from Oxnard with a whole truck bed stacked with watermelons; giant, round, striped ones that looked like they belonged in a cartoon. He parked out front like he was running a farmers market out of a 1980s pickup, and just like that, we were in the fruit business.

"Vamos a venderlas," my dad said. And that was that.

We tossed a few dozen sandías in a pile right in the front yard and slapped together a sign: "WATERMELONS 4 SALE." My sister was appointed cashier; really, she just sat on a milk crate while the rest of us went mobile.

Alfonso, David, and I found an old shopping cart; we don't even know where it came from, and filled it up with as many watermelons as it could hold before the wheels started to wobble. We hit the neighborhood like mini street hustlers, yelling "¡Sandías! ¡Sandias!" as we rolled down the cracked sidewalks of East L.A.

I think we were selling them for four bucks a pop; one dollar for each of us, and one for my dad's buddy. Not exactly a business plan, but it worked. We pushed a few loads around the block and made some quick sales. People came out in slippers and hairnets, handing over sweaty dollar bills like it was an ice cream truck.

Then came the bright idea: "Let's go up Hazard. Toward City Terrace Park."

Now if you know Hazard Avenue, you know that hill is no joke. That thing's steep like it's trying to punch your calves. We took turns pushing, sweating bullets, panting, with Alfonso pretending he was steering a lowrider while I nearly passed out behind him. The cart squeaked like it was begging us to turn around.

At the top of the hill, there's this set of old folks' apartments. We're standing there, catching our breath, and yelling "¡Saaaandías!" like street vendors in a mercado. Then, out of nowhere, an old lady leans over her balcony and yells back.

"¡Tráiganme una! Y si alguien pregunta, nomás digan que soy su abuelita."

We looked at each other, shrugged, and wheeled the cart toward the building. We piled into the tiny elevator, giggling, holding onto the watermelon like it was a sacred delivery. But of course, it stops on the wrong floor.

The doors open, and there's this old man staring at us like we broke into his living room.

"¡Oye! Get outta here! Stop playing in the elevator!"

We froze. Like statues. Little brown statues holding fruit.

Then *ding!* We slammed the door button shut and shot up to the next floor like it was a heist getaway. Heart pounding, we found our honorary grandma, dropped off the sandía, and got a handful of change.

By the time we got back down, security was already looking for us. We ran all the way home, laughing the whole time.

We didn't get rich off those sandías, but man, we earned every dollar.

Chapter 24: Mi Tío Manuel, el de las Paletas

My tío Manuel; man, he was one of our favorite uncles. The kind that showed up with a smile, a six-pack, and a bag full of frozen joy. He'd call ahead and ask, "¿Van a estar en casa?" like he was trying to schedule a meeting. But two minutes later, there he'd be, crossing the street with ice cream in one hand and beer in the other.

He always brought us paletas. Those orange creamsicles with the vanilla filling inside. The second you heard that freezer bag crinkle, you knew it was about to be a good day. Eventually, we stopped waiting for the phone call. As soon as he dialed, we'd look out the window and see him coming out of the liquor store across the street. Or we'd meet him halfway, grinning, walking up like, "Tío, ¿qué nos trajiste?"

It was hilarious, calling us from across the street like he lived in another zip code.

Tío Manuel was a hard-working man, one of those old-school types who woke up before the sun and never complained about it. He lived in the Pico-Union district and used to catch the bus to work around 4 a.m. One time, while waiting for the bus, some cholos jumped him for his wallet. Beat him bad with one of those medieval spiked flails. He ended up in the hospital. That hurt to see; someone so kind getting treated like that. He eventually passed, and we still miss him a lot. He had this simple kind of generosity, the kind that sticks with you even after the paletas are long gone.

There was this one Fourth of July when he and another one of our uncles came by. By then, Tío Manuel had a car and had finally learned how to drive. That alone was a celebration. They cracked open some beers and posted up in the front yard, laughing, reminiscing, and lighting fireworks like a couple of big kids.

Somehow because why not, a friendly firecracker war broke out. It started with throwing firecrackers and jumping jacks. Next thing we know, they're *chucking them into each other's cars.*

Tío Manuel took it to the next level and threw a whole brick of fireworks onto the roof of my other uncle's car. The thing had one of those soft vinyl tops, and it got *wrecked.* Burn holes, black streaks, and a big dent where the brick hit. Looked like a war zone.

Not to be outdone, my other uncle launched a whole pack of firecrackers *into* Manuel's car. Through the window. Boom! The inside lit up like it was the Fourth of July *inside* the car too. Seats scorched. Dash stained with smoke. The whole thing smelled like burnt plastic and regret.

After the chaos died down, they looked at their cars; blown up, charred, and smoking. Then they just looked at each other and hugged it out.

Like nothing happened.

Meanwhile, we were on the sidewalk crying with laughter, trying not to pee ourselves.

That was Tío Manuel. Always showing up with popsicles and leaving a trail of fireworks behind him. The kind of uncle that made growing up something you never forget.

Chapter 25: Ha Vale

My other tío Manuel; not the paleta one, but my dad's brother, was in a league of his own. One of the laziest guys you'd ever meet. And I say that with love. His favorite phrase, no matter the situation, was a half-hearted, shrug-it-off, can't-be-bothered: "Ha vale."

Stub your toe? "Ha vale." Lose your job? "Ha vale." End of the world? You guessed it, "Ha vale."

This guy could sniff out a cigarette from a mile away. He was like a K9, but instead of drugs, his nose was trained for Marlboros. When he used to stay at our house, you'd wake up in the morning to the smell of smoke. No bacon, no coffee, just straight cigarette.

I remember one time my mom had a stash of emergency smokes. Don't ask why she had them, but they were hidden deep in the kitchen cupboard, behind the glasses, inside a little tin box with a lid that creaked like a haunted house door. Nobody knew they were there.

Except Tío Manuel.

He found them. Like magic. Like some twisted, nicotine bloodhound. We'd walk into the kitchen and catch him in the act, tin open, cigarette in hand, lighter ready.

"¿Qué?" he'd say, "Estaban ahí, no?" followed, of course, by a classic "Ha vale."

He'd go outside and sit on the porch like a king surveying his kingdom, puffing away like it was his job. And for him, it kind of was. That, and perfecting the art of doing absolutely nothing.

But lazy as he was, there was something funny and comforting about him. The way he just didn't give a damn. The way he could turn a missing pack of smokes into a comedy skit. He might've moved slow, but he left behind stories that move fast in our memory.

Chapter 26: Oh My Dara

My tío Filo. Man, he was a character. Always cracking jokes, even when he didn't know he was doing it. One of his most legendary lines came from something so simple, so innocent, but it became part of our family vocabulary forever.

He had this white neighbor who used to say "Oh my God!" all the time. Loud, dramatic, like it was her personal catchphrase. Burnt toast? "Oh my God!" Car alarm outside? "Oh my God!" One time her sprinklers didn't go off, and she screamed it like the house was on fire.

Tío Filo didn't quite catch the phrase at first. English wasn't his strong suit, but he was always trying. So, every time she shouted "Oh my God," he'd nod and reply with a straight face: "Oh my daughter."

Except, with his accent, it came out like: "Oh my dara."

And he meant it. He wasn't trying to be funny. He legit thought that's what people said when something went wrong.

We'd be in the driveway watching this whole exchange go down. The neighbor yelling "Oh my God!" from her porch, and Tío Filo calmly waving back, "Oh my dara," like he was offering condolences at a funeral.

It got to the point where he started saying it *everywhere.*

A car backfires? "Oh my dara."

Someone drops a plate? "Oh my dara."

My cousin fell off his bike once and before we could even help him up, Tío blurts out, "Oh my dara."

We were dying.

Tío Filo never cared if he got the words right. He just rolled with it. And somehow, he ended up creating a phrase even better than the original.

And that wasn't even his best story.

He used to tell us about the times he'd go stand right in front of Los Angeles City Hall wearing a full-on Mexican kit; sombrero, huaraches, sarape draped over his shoulders like a revolutionary, just trying to get deported.

"Why pay for a plane ticket," he'd say, "when they'll send you home for free?"

Don't know if he really did do that, but I used to imagine him out there, standing there, arms crossed, waiting for immigration to roll up and do their thing.

Stories would float around of how every few months, he'd return to L.A. just long enough to collect the rent from his properties. Then, like a true legend, he'd head back to Ixtlahuacán. And that's where the real fun started.

According to him, he'd roll into the plaza like a boss, wheeling a wheelbarrow full of beer, banda following him, with the whole town following like he was the mayor. Just cruising through the plaza, music playing, bottles clinking, everyone shouting "¡Filo llegó!"

We never knew if all the stories were true, but honestly, we didn't care. It was Tío Filo. Even if half of it was made up, it was still better than most people's reality.

He didn't just live life. He paraded through it.

Chapter 27: A mi no me digas So

My parents thought "so" was a bad word. Not like a little rude or kinda disrespectful; *a straight-up bad word*. Say it loud enough and you were guaranteed a consequence. If one of us kids slipped and said, "So?" in response to anything, there were only two outcomes: a slap upside the head or "incate alli". Sometimes both.

And let me be clear, we weren't kneeling like you do in church, all calm and rested. Nope. This was *paraditos*; back straight, no leaning, no squirming. Like we were statues made out of guilt. If you tried to rest your butt on your heels, that was a time add-on. If you slouched, boom, chingaso. Sometimes they didn't even say anything, they'd just walk by and *thwap!*—a reminder to suffer with posture.

"A mí no me digas so," my mom would say, with that look that could fry your soul.

We used to laugh about it later, but in the moment? You didn't dare question it. One time Alfonso said "so" under his breath, and my mom whipped around like she had superhuman hearing.

"¿Qué dijiste?"

"Uh... I said 'slow'... like... you're going too slow."

Nice try. "Incate cabron, ten minutes". That tile was cold too, like punishment baked right into the floor.

In our house, "so" was a fightin' word. Not because it was rude, but because it sounded like attitude. And attitude didn't fly in our house unless it was from a parent. *So* we learned real quick.

Chapter 28: No Me Truenen los Dientes

I don't know if you know what I'm talking about, but it's that little "tsss" noise you make with your teeth and tongue. You know the one. That sound that says, "I'm annoyed," "I'm tired," or "You're full of it," without saying a single word.

Well, let me tell you, *that* noise didn't fly in our house.

The second you let one of those "tsss" sounds slip, my dad would snap his head around like he just heard a car alarm go off. "¿Qué fue eso?" he'd growl. And if you acted like you didn't know what he was talking about? Worse.

"¡No me truenen los dientes!" That was his line.

And you knew that if he said it with his eyebrows already raised, it was game over. You might get a chanclazo, a slap to the back of the head, or if you were really unlucky, *the stare* followed by the slow rise from the couch. And that slow rise meant he was going to take his time getting up... just to make sure you had enough time to be scared.

Sometimes we did it on accident, like just breathing out after being told to clean the yard or take out the trash. One little "tsss" under your breath and boom, chingaso.

One time Alfonso did it while standing behind him. My dad turned so fast, it was like he had sonar.

"¿Estás tronando los dientes, cabrón?"

And before Alfonso could answer, he was getting chased around the coffee table.

It became a joke later. "Tsss" became code for *I wanna say something, but I value my life.* We'd mock each other quietly, making the noise behind closed doors like we were running a rebellion.

We were very careful not to get caught saying "so," or "tsss," and we sure as hell didn't talk back.

Respect, fear, survival, it was all part of growing up in our house.

And if you forgot? Don't worry. That chingaso would remind you real quick.

Chapter 29: Superman

My mom would always remind me of this story every time I visited her. I was probably in the seventh grade when it happened, and I had this busted-up ten-speed bike, but it really only had, like, three speeds that worked. My dad came home one day with it like he was delivering treasure.

"Te traje una bicicleta," he said proudly.

"From el carnicero."

That should've been the first red flag. El Carnicero was a local wanna-be veterano who would steal cold cuts from the liquor store and come sell them to my mom at a huge discount.

The thing was a Frankenstein of a bike. Rusty frame, peeling stickers, bent handlebars and no brakes. Well, it had one brake. The front one. Which, if you've ever tried to use as your only method of stopping, you already know; it's basically a front flip waiting to happen.

One afternoon I was bored out of my mind, and my mom gave me that classic warning:

"No te vayas a subir a la bicicleta."

So, naturally, I got on the bike.

Our yard wasn't built for riding. There was a narrow winding sidewalk running from the front gate to the back, with thorny rose bushes lining one whole side like nature's version of barbed wire. I thought I could ride back and forth and keep it slow.

On like my 6th time, coming from the back, I picked up a little too much speed and tried to make the tight turn near the gate. My hands reached for the brakes and of course, the only one that worked was the front. I squeezed it.

Bad move.

Next thing I know, the back of the bike flew up, the front wheel stopped dead, and I went flying. Arms out. Straight into the rose bushes. *Sopatelas.*

I didn't even scream. I couldn't. I was more scared of my mom hearing me than the thorns shredding my arms.

I crawled out like a wounded soldier, bleeding but silent. Hid the bike, brushed off the leaves, and started pulling thorns out of my arms one by one like I was removing evidence from a crime scene.

A little while later, my mom saw me sitting on the porch, all quiet.

"¿Qué estás haciendo? ¿Por qué ya no estás jugando?"

I mumbled, "Nada… estoy cansado."

She looked at me, then cracked up.

"¡Volaste como Superman por los rosales!" she said, shaking her head.

At least she didn't hit me. I guess even she had to admit, it was kinda impressive.

Chapter 30: Sopatelas

Betty, I think that was her name. My older brother was working at the First Street Store at the time, and one night he brought two coworkers home to drink. We were living in the back house then; me and my brothers, and let's just say, privacy was minimal and the walls were, well, barely walls.

So there we are, doing our thing, and Betty heads to the restroom. A few minutes later— *¡chingaso!* A loud thud comes from behind the bathroom door. My room was right in front of the restroom, and I was just sitting there watching TV. I heard it, but I figured she slipped or dropped something. Nothing major.

The next day, we found out it was more than just a fall. There was a *hole* in the wall. Not a crack, not a dent, *a whole damn hole* between the sink and the shower. Apparently, while washing her hands, Betty lost her balance, stumbled backward, and went right through the drywall like a Kool-Aid man in heels.

We all stared at the damage, and immediately the panic set in. There was no way we could tell my dad. No way. We would've gotten the beating of the year. So, what do we do? David, in his infinite wisdom, finds this life-sized poster of a female bodybuilder; tan, flexing, totally random, and tapes it over the hole like it was some kind of weird art installation.

That poster stayed up for *years*. At some point, it just became part of the house. People would come over, look at it, and we'd be like, "Oh yeah, that's our workout inspiration."

But of course, nothing lasts forever. One day, my dad walks into the back house and starts sniffing around.

"¿Qué huele?" he says.

There was this funky smell we'd all kind of ignored, thinking it was just old-house funk or our pedos.

He walks over, peels back the poster, and boom. There it is. The infamous hole, all podrido and moldy around the edges like a science experiment gone wrong.

"¿¡Qué chingados pasó aquí!?"

I pulled the classic, "Yo no sé," and tried to disappear into the couch.

He ranted for a while, cussing under his breath, but in the end, he patched it up. Didn't even bring it up again. Maybe he was just too tired to deal with it. Or maybe even he had to admit, a bodybuilder poster covering a mystery hole was kind of legendary.

Chapter 31: Las Reinas del Fútbol

When my uncle had the soccer team, there was a day the league was planning to take official team pictures. And for that, each team had to have its own set of reinas; basically team queens to pose in the photos. Some kind of tradition, I guess.

So Rodolfos (the coach) wife, nominated their daughter Eli. And of course, my mom, *metiendo las patas,* puts Carmen down as the other reina. We didn't think anything of it at the time. They were both like ten years old, excited, nervous, dressed up like they were going to church.

They showed up that Sunday morning in sky blue dresses, little heels, hair curled, all ready for their big moment. But then we got to the field...

Every other team's reinas showed up looking like swimsuit models.

Bikini tops, tight shorts, heels higher than their standards, hair done like they were heading to a Lowrider calendar shoot.

And then there was our team, with two ten-year-olds in pastel blue looking like they were there for a primera comunion celebration.

They were the *laughing stock* of the league. Dads were pointing, snickering. Moms were throwing shade left and right.

"¡Míralas, las viejas encueradas!" the wives were whispering, all salty.

And the husbands? "Míralas, las Viejas encueradas!, full of excitement.

Meanwhile, Eli and Carmen stood there, smiling awkwardly for the camera while looking like they wanted to melt into the grass.

Chapter 32: Caramelo

If you grew up in East L.A. in the 80s, chances are you've heard of Caramelo. Hell, he probably cut your hair if you were a dumbass, that is.

Caramelo worked out of that $4 barbershop on Cesar Chavez and Eastman. Classic spot, faded barber poles, sun-faded posters of 80s haircuts no one asked for anymore, and a row of beat-up vinyl chairs that made your butt stick in the summer. When we were in junior high, Caramelo wasn't even cutting hair yet. He was the broom guy, sweeping up hair like he was training for the big leagues.

Then one day, I walk in and there he is, scissors in hand, calling out, "¡Véngase, jefe!" like he was the head barber. I looked around like, "Who let this guy graduate from broom to blade?"

That shop had a system. Everyone knew the guy in the first chair was *the guy*. Always a long-ass line for him. Meanwhile, Caramelo's chair? Empty. Like haunted-house empty. People would walk in, take one look at Caramelo waving them over, and say, "Nah, I'll wait."

But every once in a while, some poor soul who didn't know better would take the bait. They'd sit in Caramelo's chair like it was no big deal, and that's when it happened.

Everyone in the shop would smirk. Heads would turn. You'd hear the quiet chuckles. That's how you knew, this fool was new.

Fifteen minutes later, the guy would look in the mirror and freeze. Line-up crooked. Fade patchy. One side higher than the other. Hairline looking like a topographical map. That's when realization hit: *that's* why he had no line.

Caramelo meant well. But that didn't mean he was good. And that name, Caramelo, just made it worse. You couldn't even complain with a straight face. "Who messed you up?" "Caramelo."

East L.A. legend. And cautionary tale.

Chapter 33: Our Room

I remember when we were kids growing up in a two-bedroom house. Well, *technically* one bedroom and a makeshift shack in the back, but in East Los, that's still a bedroom. In our neighborhood, everything could be a bedroom. The laundry room? Bedroom. The living room? Bedroom. Dining room? Throw down a mattress, boom, bedroom.

Me and my two brothers slept in the shack. I mean "bedroom." This room was smaller than a handicapped toilet stall. Somehow, we squeezed in a set of bunk beds, and David slept on one of those old-school fold-up cots. We actually thought that cot was a real bed back then. Deluxe.

Alfonso slept on the top bunk, but he couldn't even sit up straight without banging his head on the ceiling. Did I mention the ceiling was barely six feet high? No insulation. None. You stick a nail through that ceiling and it pokes out the roof like a flagpole.

But don't feel bad for us, we were the lucky ones. Carmen had to share a room with my parents… until she "upgraded" to her own room: the living room.

And even though we were packed in like tamales, we still found ways to make it fun. We played hide and seek in there. Yes, *hide and seek* in a space barely big enough to turn around in.

We'd make teams. One team hid, the other counted outside the door. But instead of just tagging the other team, you had to hit them with a chancla. That was the rule. If one of your team members made it out the door without getting hit, you got to hide again.

And you're probably wondering *where the hell did you hide?*

Anywhere and everywhere. On the window sill, under the bed, in a Veliz, between the bed and the wall hugging the post like you were part of the frame, even above the door, holding on to the top bunk like some chancla-dodging Spider-Man.

You had to walk into our room sideways. Two steps in and you ran straight into the bunk bed. But to us, it was a castle, a jungle gym, a war zone. It was ours.

Chapter 3: Mismatched and Mole

Growing up, we didn't have fancy dish sets or matching silverware. What we had was... eclectic. A fork from here, a spoon from there, and plates that looked like they came from garage sales across three decades. The only things that matched in our whole kitchen were the glass cups and not because we bought them in a set. Nope. They were all old mole Doña María jars, scrubbed and repurposed like crystal goblets.

As punishment or maybe just to make sure we looked presentable, my mom would hand me a jar and say, "Quítale la etiqueta." I'd be standing at the sink, peeling soggy paper off glass like it was my job. All so when company came over, they wouldn't know our glasses once held spicy mole.

And let's talk about the plates. We didn't buy them, we earned them. One Shakey's buffet at a time. My mom had a system. Every time we ate at Shakey's, she'd discreetly slide a salad plate into her oversized purse. "Para que tengamos un juego," she'd whisper, like it was a noble mission. After enough visits, we had a semi-matching set. And not just plates, we even took the pizza pans. Yup. Straight off the table, crust crumbs and all.

It sounds ridiculous now, but back then, it made sense. We weren't stealing; we were surviving. And hey, we had pizza pans that lasted longer than some of our furniture.

It might not have been fancy, but it worked.

That kitchen was filled with mismatched love and mole memories.

Made in the USA
Middletown, DE
24 April 2025

74666786R00051